Drawing Is Awesome!

DRAWING AWESOME SEA CREATURES

Damien Toll

WINDMILL
BOOKS

Contents

Introduction

Drawing is a fun and rewarding hobby for children and adults alike. This book is designed to show how easy it is to draw great pictures by building them in simple stages.

What you will need

Only basic materials are required for effective drawing. These are:

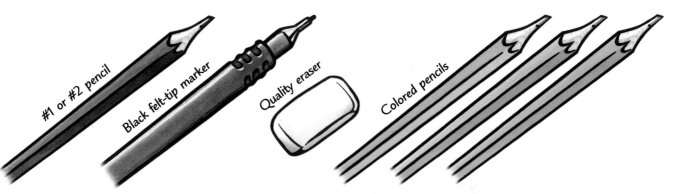

#1 or #2 pencil

Black felt-tip marker

Quality eraser

Colored pencils

These will be enough to get started. Avoid buying the cheapest pencils. Their leads often break off in the sharpener, even before they can be used. The leads are also generally too hard, making them difficult to see on the page.

Cheap erasers also cause problems by smudging rather than erasing. This often leaves a permanent stain on the paper. By spending a little more on art supplies in these areas, problems such as these can be avoided.

When purchasing a black marker, choose one to suit the size of your drawings. If you draw on a large scale, a thick felt-tip marker may be necessary. If you draw on a medium scale, a medium-point marker will do and if on a small scale, a 0.3 mm, 0.5 mm, 0.7 mm, or 0.8 mm felt-tip marker will work best.

The Stages

Simply follow the lines drawn in orange on each stage using your #1 or #2 pencil. The blue lines on each stage show what has already been drawn in the previous stages.

1.

2.

3.

In the final stage the drawing has been outlined in black and the simple shape and wire-frame lines erased. The shapes are only there to help us build the picture. We finish the picture by drawing over the parts we need to make it look like our subject with the black marker, and then erasing all the simple shape lines.

4.

Included here is a sketch of the surgeonfish as it would be originally drawn by an artist.

These are how all the animals in this book were originally worked out and drawn. The orange and blue stages you see above are just a simplified version of this process. The drawing here has been made by many quick pencil strokes working over each other to make the line curve smoothly. It does not matter how messy it is as long as the artist knows the general direction of the line to follow with the black marker at the end. The pencil lines are erased and a clean outline is left. Therefore, do not be afraid to make a little mess with your #1 or #2 pencil, as long as you do not press so hard that you cannot erase it afterwards.

5.

Grids made of squares are set behind each stage in this book. Make sure to draw a grid lightly on your page so it does not press into the paper and show up after being erased. Artist tips have also been added to show you some simple things that can make your drawing look great. Have fun!

The Shark

Sharks are fish. There are over 300 varieties of shark. Some are only a few inches long and some grow to be over 20 feet (6 m) long. The smaller sharks eat plankton while the bigger sharks eat fish, squid, octopuses, and seals. Sharks do not have bones, but a skeleton made out of cartilage.

1.

Draw a grid with four equal squares going across and three down.

Draw a pointy egg in the left half of the grid. Notice the angle this egg shape is on.

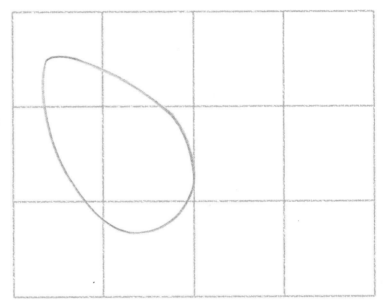

2.

Add a large fin towards the bottom of the egg shape reaching down to the lower left corner of the grid.

Draw a hook that flows off the rear of the egg shape. This will be the shark's lower body.

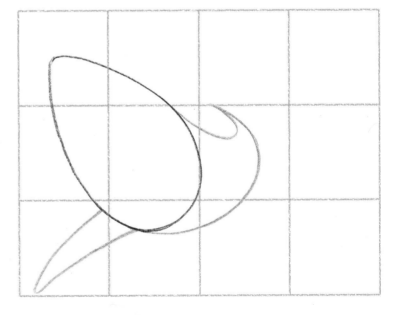

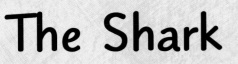

3.

Add the dorsal fin on top of the shark. Be careful to put it in the correct place on the grid. Draw in the four gills near the rear of the egg shape.

Draw the other fin, which goes almost all the way to the right edge of the grid. Add the rear fin behind the right fin.

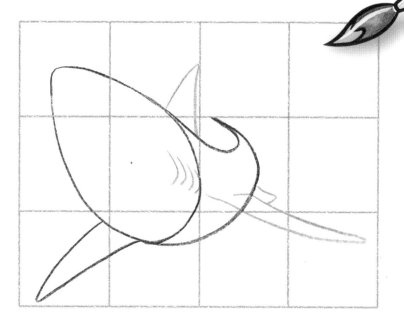

4.

Draw a curved line from the nose to the top of the first gill. Then draw a small line from the bottom of the last gill to the right fin, and from the right fin around the body. This will separate the colors.

Draw two spots for the nose. Draw in the eye. Put in a shape like an upside down moon for the mouth and add teeth to the top and bottom.

Draw the tall tail and bottom section behind the dorsal fin.

5.

Outline your shark and erase the pencil. You can color your shark gray, dark green or blue.

The Dolphin

The dolphin is a member of the whale family. They are warm-blooded and breathe air from the surface. Out of the 30 species of dolphins, the bottlenose dolphin is the most common. They live and travel in big groups called pods. Dolphins love to play and will often jump out of the water and perform various flips.

1.

Draw a grid with four equal squares going across and three down.

Draw in the shape for the body of the dolphin. Even though this shape is long, notice how it is stubby at the front and more stretched out at the back.

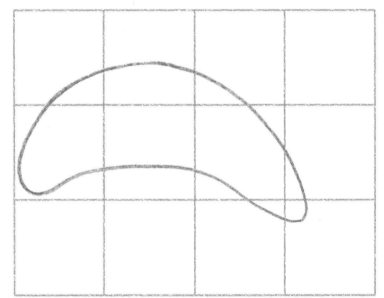

2.

Add the beak at the bottom of the body shape.

Draw a dorsal fin above the right-hand side of the center of the body shape. Add the tail to finish this stage.

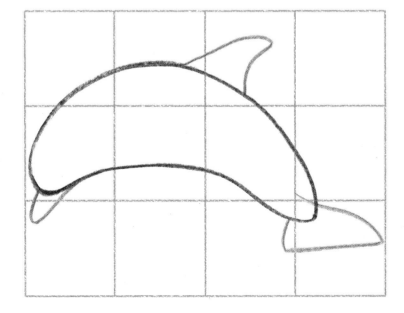

3.

Split the beak shape in half with a line for the mouth. Draw in the eye and cheek top. Add the pectoral fins.

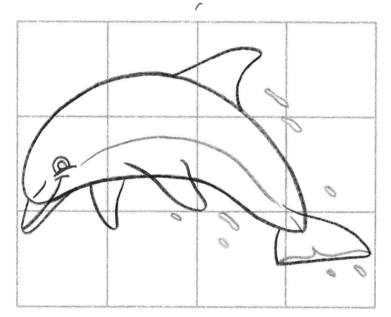

4.

Draw a line along and below the center of the dolphin's body. Add some water droplets to show that it is leaping out of the water.

5.

Outline your drawing and erase the pencil lines. We have made this dolphin grey and added highlight points around it to make it look shiny.

The Sea Turtle

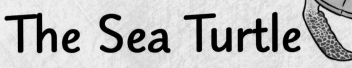

Sea turtles are cold-blooded and live in the warmer parts of the world's oceans. Sea turtles do not have feet but have flippers for swimming. Most of a sea turtle's life is spent in the ocean. They do come to land to lay eggs. On the beach, the female will dig a hole and lay many eggs. When the babies hatch, they make their way back to the ocean.

1.

Draw a grid with four equal squares going across and three down.

Draw a circle for the head in the top left square of the grid. Draw in the shape for the shell.

Notice the wire-frame line between the head and the shell. If this line was carried through the head and shell, it would show that the whole drawing is based in this direction.

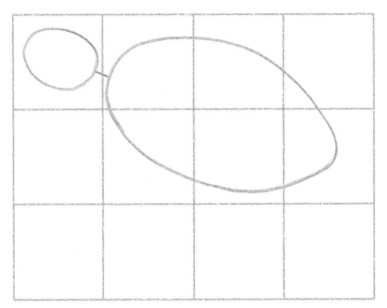

2.

Draw the beak on the head circle. Join the head to the shell at the top. Draw in the neck and large flipper on the underside.

Add the back flippers. Notice the flipper on top is slightly smaller than the one on the bottom.

Draw in the shape for the eye.

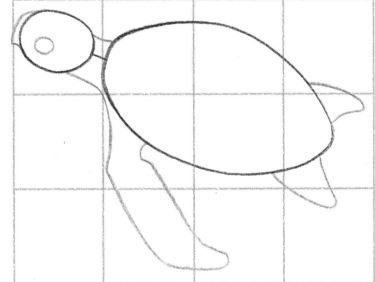

3.

Look closely on the grid to see where the shell pattern falls. The hexagonal shapes are not in the middle of the shell, but are more towards the top side. This makes the shell look three dimensional.

Draw in the leaf-shaped eye to finish this stage.

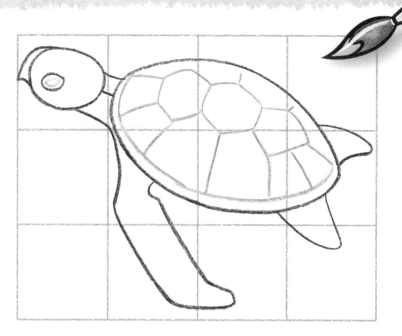

Artist Tip:

The head and flippers have many shapes on them. If we drew them all in with our outline marker, it would darken the picture too much. This is because things in life are rarely colored black. See how dark the drawing to the right is with too many detailed shapes done with an outline marker. When using your marker, try to limit the detail of your subject.

Notice how some of the outlines for the pattern on the turtle's shell do not go right to the edge or meet up with each other. This is another way of limiting detail.

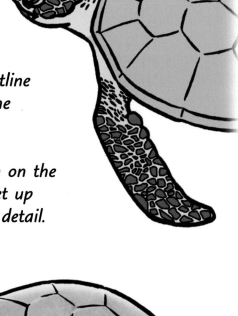

4.

Outline your turtle and color. The head and flippers have blue shapes covering them. The shell is mostly green with a little blue lightly mixed in, in patches.

Pelican

Pelicans are big majestic birds. Their wingspan can reach over six feet (2 m) in length. They also have a very long beak which they use to scoop up fish out of the water to eat. They float very well and have webbed feet for paddling. Pelicans are found in warm parts of the world. They nest in trees and sometimes on the ground.

1.

Draw a grid with four equal squares going across and three down.

Study the shape for the body. It has a long slope going up and a shorter steeper slope going down. Draw this in on the correct place on your grid.

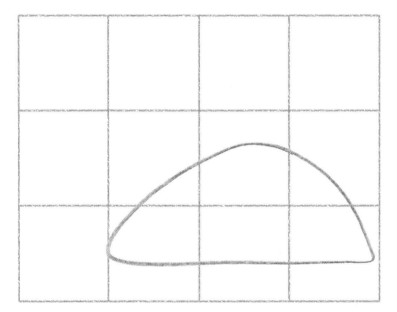

2.

Draw the shape for the wing inside the body shape.

Draw a shape for the head near the top of the grid. Draw two curved lines for the neck, merging it into the body.

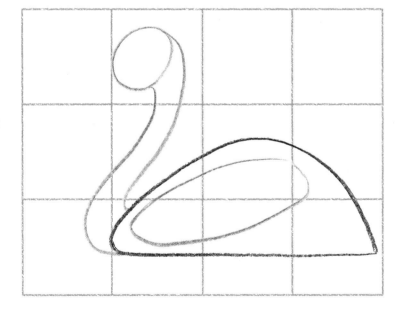

3.

Add the beak onto the head shape. Draw in the eye and whiskers on the back of the head.

Draw a zig-zag line and some straight lines for the feathers on the bottom of the wing shape.

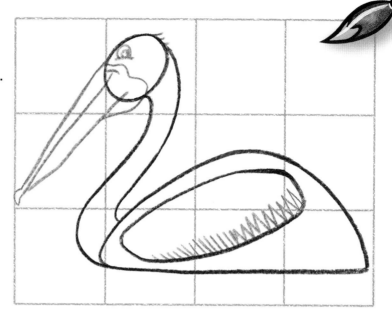

4.

Draw the jagged lines on its back for the rough feathers. Add some more jagged lines going across from the wing to the rear of the body.

Put in some water ripples to finish this stage.

5.

Outline your pelican and erase the pencil lines. Most pelicans are black and white. We have used a gray pencil to shade some of the white areas.

Clownfish

There are many different types of clownfish. This is the percula clownfish, which is the most well known. They live in tropical areas of the world where the water is warm. The clownfish's friend is the anemone. It has long tentacles that the clownfish hides in. These tentacles kill and eat other fish but the clownfish has built up an immunity to its sting.

1.

Draw a grid with four equal squares going across and three down.

Draw in an oval shape that is pointier at the rear. Make sure the oval is slanted in an upwards direction.

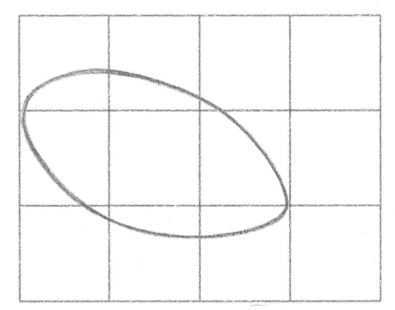

2.

Add on the dorsal fins on top of the body shape. Notice how they start in the second square from the left of the grid. Draw on the surrounding fins and add the tail.

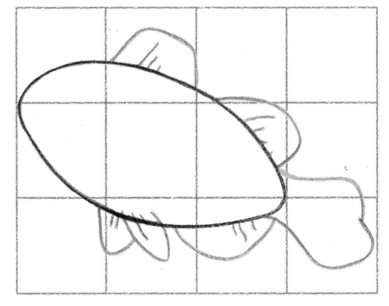

3.

Draw a mouth that looks like a stretched "S" on its side. Draw in the eye and add a curved line above it for the brow.

Add the pectoral fin in the middle of the body. Note the large size of the pectoral fin.

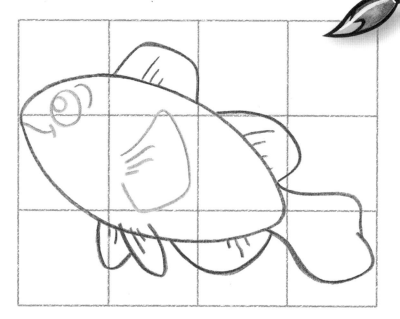

4.

Add three stripes. These surround the head, fall behind the dorsal fins and circle the tail.

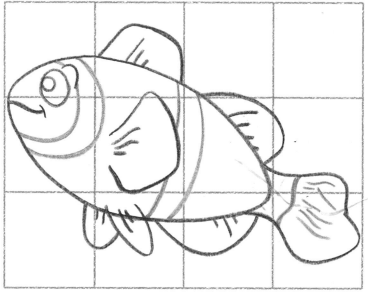

5.

Outline your artwork and erase the pencil lines. Color your clownfish.

Sea Horse

Sea horses are fish. They do not have scales but have skin stretched over their bony skeleton. Sea horses are found in the shallow, warmer parts of the ocean. The fin located on their back propels them through the water in a standing position.

1.

Draw a grid with two equal squares going across and four down.

First, draw the oval-shaped head in the top left of the grid. Draw in the body shape, being careful to place it slightly slanted to the right.

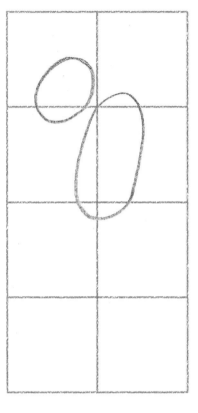

2.

Draw on the snout and neck. Notice how they flow onto the head and body shape. Draw in the twisting tail.

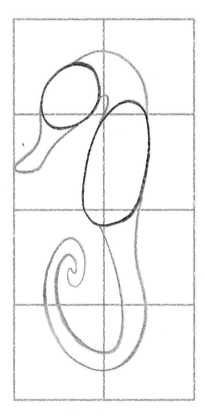

3.

Add the shape on top of the head and the points on the back, running from the top of the neck to the tip of the tail. Draw in the eye and pupil.

Draw slightly curved lines going horizontally across the body of the seahorse from the neck to the end of the tail. These represent the bony skeleton.

Draw a line down the length of the sea horse, curved between each previously drawn horizontal skeletal line. Add another vertical line towards the front of its body.

Draw in the little fin underneath the belly and the large fin on the back.

4.

Outline your drawing and erase the pencil. Sea horses come in many different colors and patterns. You may like to try making up your own color pattern.

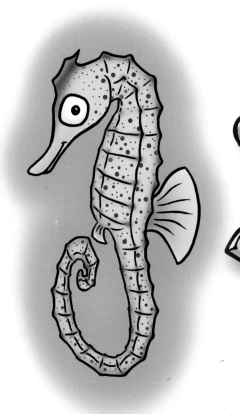

Octopus

The octopus is a master of disguise. It can change its color to mirror its surroundings so it cannot be seen. This camouflage helps it hide from predators. It has great eyesight and can squeeze through very small gaps between rocks to escape.

1.

Draw a grid with four equal squares going across and three down.

Draw a shape for the head in the top right side of the grid. Draw another shape slightly smaller under this for the body.

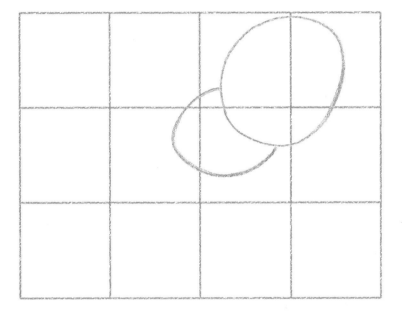

2.

Draw in some curved lines for legs. Be careful to note how and where they fall on the grid.

3.

Draw in the top side of the legs, bringing the tips to a point.

Add the eyes. One of them is outside the head shape and one is inside the head shape. Make the head a little pointier.

4.

Add some suckers to the underside of the legs.

5.

Outline your octopus with your marker and erase the pencil lines. You can color your octopus any color you like as they can mimic every color.

The Crab

Crabs are ten-legged crustaceans that walk sideways. They have two large claws called pincers which they use for feeding or to defend themselves if necessary. All their bones are on the outside. This is called an exoskeleton. There are more than 5000 species of crabs. Some live in the ocean and some live on land.

1.

Draw a grid with four equal squares going across and three down.

First, draw in an oval for the crab's body. Draw in two more shapes pointing down and towards the center of the grid. These will be the pincers.

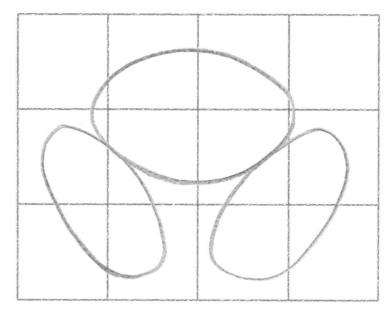

2.

Add a shape that is wide at the top and comes to a point for the legs on either side of the body shape.

Join the pincer shapes to the body at their tops, below the leg shape we have just drawn. Draw a curved line on both of the pincers.

Draw a curved line through and just under the middle of the oval for the body.

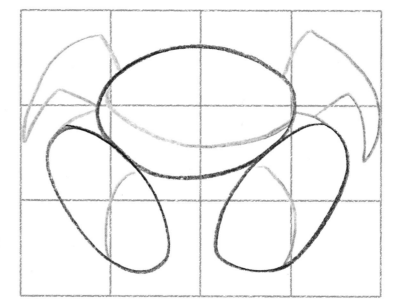

3.

Break the legs shapes up into three legs using two lines on each.

Add the eyes above the middle line in the oval body shape. Draw the mouth parts under this line.

Define the pincers.

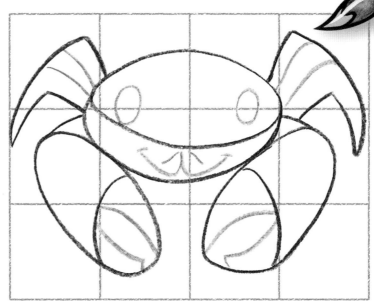

4.

Put joints in on the legs. Draw a small hump at the top of the oval for the body shape. Draw in the parts underneath the eye.

Draw in a line to make the bottom of the shell and pincer arms.

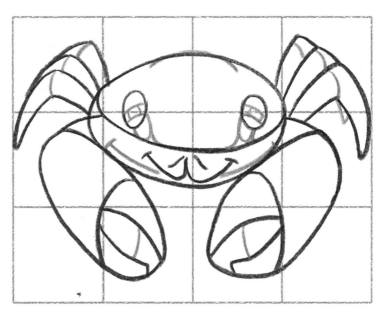

5.

Outline your crab with your marker and erase the pencil lines. Color your crab.

The Penguin

Penguins are birds. They cannot fly through the air but they do "fly" through the water with their flippers. Penguins hatch from eggs like other birds. They are only found below the equator and like to swim in icy cold seas.

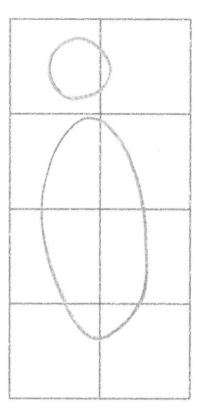

1.

Draw a grid with two equal squares going across and four down.

Draw the head shape in the correct position on the grid. Draw the body shape and move on to stage two.

2.

Draw the beak on the front of the head shape. Draw in the eye and the mouth.

Draw in the neck, which flows onto the head and body shapes. Draw the puffy legs at the bottom of the body shape.

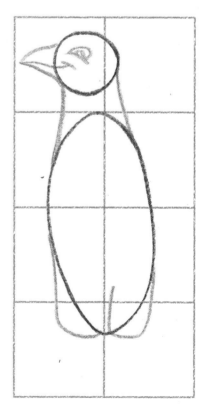

3.

Draw in the flippers (or wings) around the middle of the belly.

Draw a line from the neck to the flipper. Then continue it down to the back of the leg. Draw in the feet and a little bit for the tail.

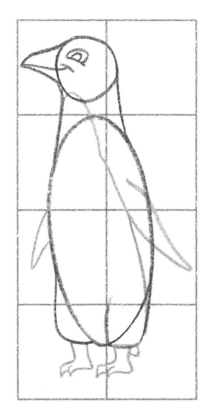

4.

Outline your penguin and color as you like.

Killer Whale

The killer whale is a large marine mammal that hunts for its prey. They hunt in groups and eat fish, squid, seals, penguins, and other whales. They have a white underbelly and a white patch behind the eye and near the tail. They can grow to over 26 feet (8 m) long and weigh over three and a half tons. The dorsal fin of a male can reach almost 6½ feet (2 m) tall.

1.

Draw a grid with four equal squares going across and two down.

Begin with a shape on the lower part of the grid. This will represent the killer whale's body.

2.

Draw the pointy but still rounded nose of the whale, being careful to merge it onto the body shape.

Draw the dorsal fin to the rear of the body shape. Add the shape for the rear of the body.

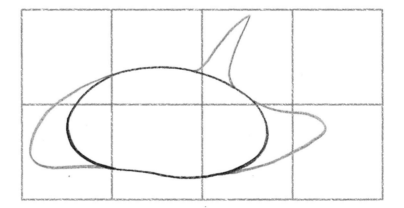

3.

Draw a little lip on the nose of the whale and continue that line for the mouth. Draw the bottom part of the lip and merge it into the nose.

Draw a wavy line through to the rear of the body for the markings. Add the short, stubby flipper.

Draw the tail fin shape.

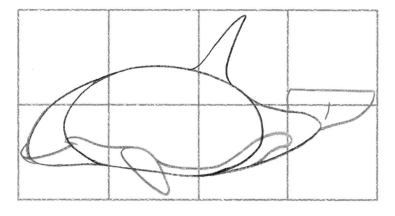

4.

Draw the eye and the marking behind it for the patch of white. Define the tail inside the shape drawn in the last stage.

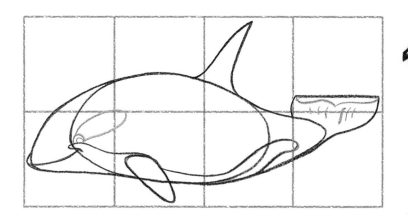

5.

Outline your work and erase the pencil lines. Killer whales are black on top. We have highlighted this to add a three-dimensional look to it. The belly has been shaded with a gray on the underside.

The Marlin

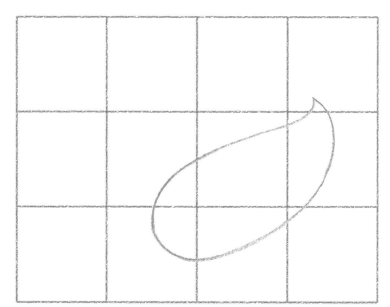

The marlin is a big, fast-swimming fish that lives offshore in deep waters. Marlin eat tuna, which are also very fast swimmers. The marlin has a long bill which it uses to stun the fish once it has caught it. It then turns around and eats it. It will also eat squid and large crustaceans. Marlin grow to be over 13 feet (4 m) long and weigh nearly a ton.

1.

Draw a grid with four equal squares going across and three down.

Begin with a shape that looks like a bent teardrop. Make sure this is positioned correctly on the grid as the bill is long and takes up a lot of room.

2.

Draw the bill so that it merges with the front of the teardrop and almost reaches the bottom left corner of the grid.

Draw the flipper that reaches to the right-hand edge of the grid. Add a curved tail end from the point of the teardrop.

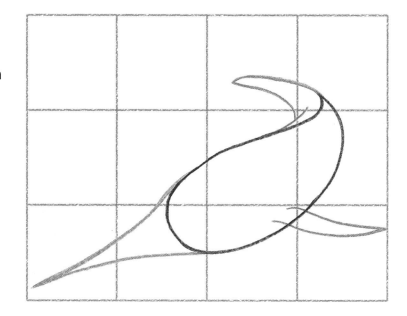

3.

Draw the mouth inside the shape for the bill. Add gill lines behind the mouth.

Draw the dorsal fin near the top of the teardrop, reaching along it to the point. Draw the tail fins on the curved tail section.

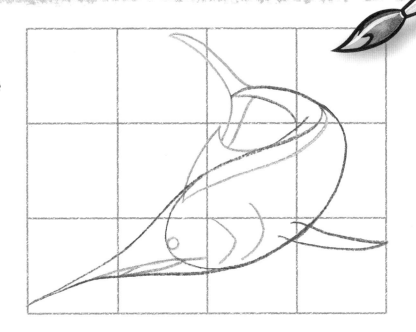

4.

Draw a thick line that stretches from the bill right through to just below the point of the teardrop. Draw in the fin on the other side of the body and the fins near the tail.

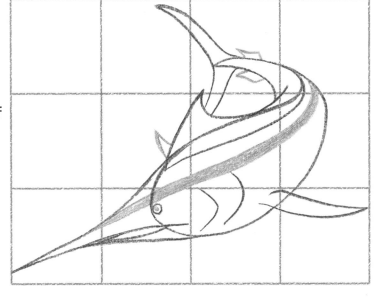

5.

Outline your marlin and erase the pencil lines. Marlin range from green to blue in their coloration. Their sides and undersides range from white to silver. They have gray colored stripes that run vertically along the body.

The Whale

This is a sperm whale. The sperm whale is very large and has a distinctive shape. Its nose is flat, not pointy like most whales. It is the largest whale to have teeth and uses these to eat giant squid. Diving very deep in the ocean where it is completely dark, the whale uses sonar to locate its prey. The sperm whale can stay underwater for up to an hour before it needs to breathe again.

1.

Draw a grid with four equal squares going across and two down.

Start with what looks like a stretched jelly bean at the left hand side of the grid. Check that your shape looks just like this one before moving on to the next stage.

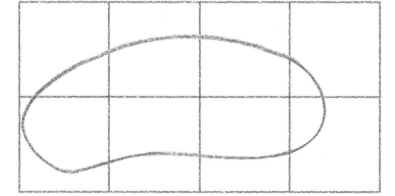

2.

Add the bottom jaw below the shape. Notice it starts from around the middle of the first shape. Draw in the eye slightly to the right and above it.

Draw in the fin and a hook shape for the lower end of its body. Draw in the bottom of a semicircle capped with a line for the tail.

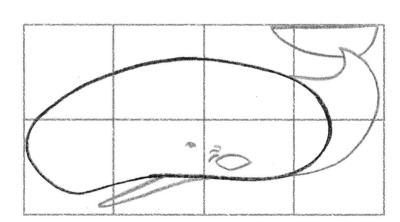

3.

Draw dorsal fins on the hook of the body. There are three fin lumps on this whale. Define the tail in the capped semicircle.

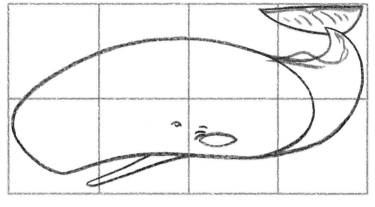

Artist Tip:

Adding a few different-sized bubbles here and there is a great way of making things look like they are underwater. A wavy line with a few dots can make up the sand. Some seaweed and a couple of rocks can finish off the ocean floor. Keep background lines very simple. That way the object of the picture, the whale, stands out.

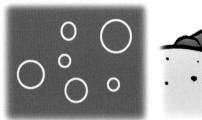

4.

The sperm whale is a whitish-gray color. In the water it can appear blue.

Surgeonfish

The blue-tailed surgeonfish is a tropical fish that can be found along the eastern coast of Australia. They grow to be over 1.5 feet (0.5 m) long and have very small scales. They live in warm shallow water and coral reefs. Surgeonfish travel in schools and graze on algae, but will sometimes eat plankton.

1.

Draw a grid with four equal squares going across and two down.

Begin with a shape that looks like an egg on its side for the body shape.

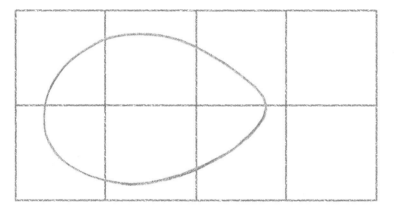

2.

Draw in the mouth parts and add lines joining them back onto the body shape. Draw the squarish fin inside the body shape. Add the tail on the point of the egg-like body shape.

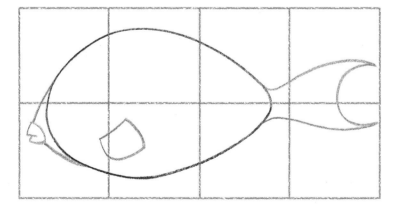

3.

Draw a curved line from the mouth up into the body shape. Draw in the eye.

Add long fins onto the outside of the body shape. These extend right through to the tail.

Draw in the diamond shape at the rear of the body. Finish with strokes and dots on the tail.

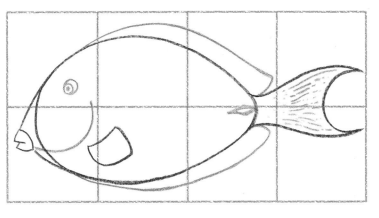

Artist Tip:

Merging means bringing two lines into one line smoothly. Notice how the lines for the front of the fish's face flow smoothly into the oval for the fish's body shape. Also, the beak and neck of the penguin merge smoothly onto both its head and body shape. You will notice that most of the shapes in this book have lines that merge into them.

Face line   Body shape   Merged into one line

4.

Outline your artwork and erase the pencil lines. Color your surgeonfish with green, bright blue, and yellow.

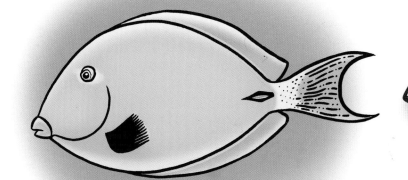

The Walrus

Large and strong, the walrus powers its way through the sea. It dives deep to the ocean floor in search of clams, snails, worms, and crustaceans to eat. It surfaces and makes its way onto land where it sunbathes with friends. The walrus has two very long tusks, which it uses to drag itself along on land and to defend itself against predators.

1.

Draw a grid with three equal squares going across and down.

Draw a circle right of the middle of the grid for the head. Draw the body shape which begins at the left side of the head circle. Check to make sure your shape is the same as this one.

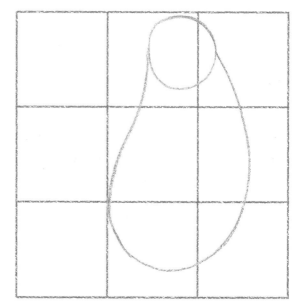

2.

Draw a circle slightly to the left and a little lower than the first head circle, but about the same size. This will be the snout.

Draw the lower body shape, making sure to merge it onto the original body shape.

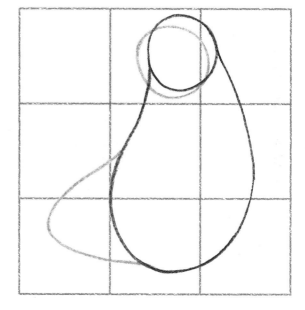

3.

Draw in the nose, which looks like a sideways "B," slightly to the left of the middle in the top of the snout circle.

Divide the cheeks in the snout circle with a line and draw in the long tusks. Draw in the front legs and fins. Add the back fin to finish this stage.

4.

Draw the eye and eyebrow on the top right of the head circle. Add whisker spots to the cheeks and a line to define the chin.

Separate the fins with some lines and add the crease on the back.

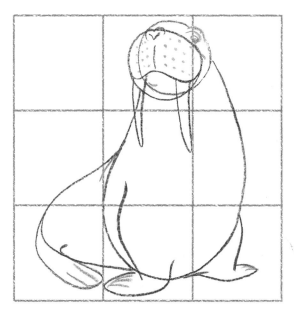

5.

Once you have outlined the picture and erased the pencil, put in a few selective whiskers coming from the whisker spots. Do not put too many in as it will darken the drawing too much.

Published in 2015 by **Windmill Books,**
an Imprint of Rosen Publishing,
29 East 21st Street, New York, NY 10010.

Written and illustrated by Damien Toll.
With thanks to Jared Gow.

Library of Congress Cataloging-in-Publication Data
Toll, Damien.
 Drawing awesome sea creatures / Damien Toll.
    pages cm. — (Drawing is awesome!)
 Includes index.
ISBN 978-1-4777-5464-1 (pbk.)
ISBN 978-1-4777-5482-5 (6 pack)
ISBN 978-1-4777-5467-2 (library binding)
1. Marine animals in art—Juvenile literature.
2. Drawing—Technique—Juvenile literature.
I. Title. NC781.T65 2015
 743.6—dc23
                                        2014027088

Manufactured in the United States of America

CPSIA Compliance Information: Batch # CW15WM: For Further Information contact
Rosen Publishing, New York, New York at 1-800-237-9932